The White Bird

The White Bird

First Edition

Copyright © 2013 William Bernhardt

Published by Balkan Press

All rights reserved

ISBN: 978-0615835488

The White Bird

and other poems by

William Bernhardt

Other Books by William Bernhardt

Fiction

Challengers of the Dust
The Code of Buddyhood
Dark Eye
The Midnight Before Christmas
Final Round

Nemesis: The Final Case of Eliot
Ness
Double Jeopardy
Strip Search
The Game Master

The Ben Kincaid Novels

Primary Justice
Blind Justice
Deadly Justice
Perfect Justice
Cruel Justice
Naked Justice
Extreme Justice
Dark Justice
Silent Justice
Murder One

Criminal Intent
Hate Crime
Death Row
Capitol Murder
Capitol Threat
Capitol Conspiracy
Capitol Offense
Capitol Betrayal
Justice Returns

Nonfiction

Story Structure: The Key to Successful Fiction
Creating Character: Bringing Your Story to Life
Perfecting Plot: Charting the Hero's Journey
The Fundamentals of Fiction (Video)

For Young Readers

Equal Justice: The Courage of Ada Lois Sipuel (biography)
Princess Alice and the Dreadful Dragon (illus. by Kerry McGhee)
The Black Sentry
Shine

Edited by William Bernhardt

Legal Briefs

Natural Suspect

For my teachers and my students:
I have learned from all of you.

Between my finger and my thumb
The squat pen rests; snug as a gun.

from "Digging"
by Seamus Heaney

Contents

Scratches

This is how it begins:
scratches on signs, on blocks
on a white page. Then the
scratches start to dance. They
recombinate, they collect sounds
they call your name.
Like so much in childhood
they are ciphers, full of secrets
but once you learn the dance
the mysteries of this world
and more, are revealed.
You learn to read.

You learn:
manners from Goldilocks
curiosity from George
gluttony from Peter
nonsense from Alice.
You set sail with Jim Hawkins, raft with Huck
and row with Mole.
Love is eternal, Catherine tells you
But so is madness, says the first Mrs. Rochester.
Jeeves helps you laugh
poetry helps you cry
Atticus shows you how to do both, with courage.

Not only have the scratches shaped the world
they have shaped your world.
They have taught you how to see.
Now you need never be afraid.

Now you will never be alone.
In the darkest night
in the deepest solitude
the scratches will call to you.
You will open the covers.
They will reach out their arms and say,
You thought you were the only one?

The Professor

In the beginning there was the Word
and the Word became my life.
When I left Pittsburgh as a boy
I had no idea what it meant
to read, to write, to teach
to compete
but I learned.
I wrote a love poem to woo my lady
and she agreed she would be mine
if I would give up writing poetry.

I go to class armed with my quotations, my books
and my bow tie
but I spend the summers writing
four books in forty years.
What does it matter if anyone has read them
or even reviewed them?
They are good books
and I have poured the strength and soul
of so many summers into them.
Haven't I earned a little recognition?
Haven't I at least earned a footnote
in the dissertation
of the next young man from Pittsburgh?

Blessings

After he carves the turkey I
lead the group giving thanks
like an acceptance speech
at the Oscars.

I'd like to thank TLF for
    teaching me how to love
    in the back seat of my father's white Cadillac
Harry, for teaching me strength
Mother, for teaching me how to dress
    don't I look sharp in my Armani tux
    with the stud instead of a bow tie?
I'd like to thank Joe Blades for
    liking my stories even
    the stupid ones
and all the little people
    who are actually huge
    Readers out in Readerland
    who make it all possible
    by reading my books even
    the stupid ones
and that librarian who first shoved a book
    into my myopic view
I'd like to thank everyone who lends my life spice
    you know who you are
I want to thank—Wait! Don't
    start the music yet
    I'm not finished.
--the carver, for teaching me
    who I didn't want to be

Alice, for teaching me
    who I did want to be
Ralph, for reminding me who I was.

A groundswell of applause begins
    but I bat it down with my hands.

Most of all, I want to thank
    the people gathered around this table
    we are all hurting
    but at least today we are all hurting together.

Mystery Story

Every now and again I catch
a glimpse of myself
we all do it
a fleeting reflection in a store window
a mirror where a wall should be
who is that squinty-eyed

idiot looking back at me
hunched shoulders, giraffe neck
receding hairline he's
all forehead and face with
eyes narrowed by reading and

time. You are old, Father William
and no starvation diet will erase
lines not etched by
laughter. I need a theme

song and I'm hoping for Over
the Rainbow but I'm hearing
What Kind of Fool Am I?

Shambhala

I emerge from a liquid sleep
and rise to the first splinter of light.
The morning sky is an unblemished canopy

its color reflected in my eyes.
The morning sun embraces the mountainside
while a fierce wind threatens to send our canvas castle

plummeting to sea level 8000 feet below.
The clouds are a wispy stair step, parallel, not ascendant,
inviting me to explore what lies beyond.

We are reliably informed
that Shambhala was a mythic city where people
strove to live a more harmonious life.

This was interspersed with more practical information—
don't feed the mythic bears—
because writers are susceptible to illusion.

But where lies illusion when clouds beckon?
Why have we come from all points of the compass?
Why would anyone climb the mountain

or traverse the winding path to the stupa,
or synagogue, or cathedral, or sit cross-legged
attending to our breathing, and why

would we ever pick up a pen to write
except to discover something far more real

and less treacherous

something beyond the brindled clouds
something you feel in your heart
something you see in the deepest sleep

and is no illusion?

Fog

The coastline is shrouded by fog
invisible but omnipresent
shifting the colors to a grayer scale
muting the conversation of the birds
preventing the sun from elucidating the morning.

We sit at a fork in the river, a crossroads
but unlike my good friend Bobby Frost
we will probably not choose the road less traveled.

The kayakers do.
They are all young women
and they glide down the shimmering water
like beings from an ice planet, a world in which surface tension
has not yet been invented.
Stroke left, stroke right, left, right, left.

The swans take no notice.
Together, the kayakers and the
gliding as-it-turns-out-not ducks
beckon me toward the alternate path
the direction this boat surely will not take.

The woman at dinner last night thought me a great iconoclast
but my choices were all made a long time ago
and though it may seem to others that I am swimming with swans
I know that I am merely cruising
on the boat I boarded when I was young
and didn't know any better.

What lies to the left?
Beneath the bridge and beyond the horizon?
Serenity, I choose to imagine.
A sense of peace with one's self.
The respect of one and all, perhaps
even the admiration of one's children.
Your work stands and salutes you as you pass by
and at night you snuggle
not with a drink, or a crossword,
but with someone soft and all-embracing
who never tires of telling you how much you matter.

The kayakers are gone now.
The swans have drifted to the midpoint
of the fork in the river.
Perhaps they will follow me whichever way I travel.
Perhaps it is much the same down either stream
never having enough, always smelling
the flowers that bloom on the other bank.

But I miss the kayak girls who veered left
without hesitation or deliberation
and now have disappeared
into the infinite recesses of the fog.

Joslyn's Idea

translucent like the
window pane like the truth and
just as hard to hold

I like slick words that
glide off the tongue and make me
sound much smarter than I

actually am. It
shimmers like heat off the road
just as hard to hold

sometimes I wish I
could shimmer, dissolve
and be translucent like

Meditation 7:15

Nothing is ever what you imagine it will be
you think, as you travel down the winding road
and catch your first glimpse of the brown ground
and the melting snow. The mountain steps aside
to reveal the nesting valley, tall pines--
perhaps not so tall as you envisioned--
pink mud and a baby blanket sky,
jazzy triangular pennants, the fierce
banshee wind, the revenants
of extinct lifeforms, and the alabaster peak
that always seems just a few more feet away.

You close your eyes and let this
imprint itself on your memory engrams,
less paradisiacal than you dreamt but more real,
more of the air you breathe and the people you know,
consumed by the collective craving for connection.

The food is pretty much what you imagined,
but not the dinner conversation, not
the deer vaulting into the forest as if
choreographed by Balanchine, not
the black-and-white bird that will not tell you its name, not
the gravity of silence, not
the carnival of consciousness left to its own devices.

Nothing is ever what you imagine it will be
and therein lies the impetus because otherwise
why would we even lace up our shoes?

Dinah and Me

My cat hates my girlfriend
and the one before her, and the one
before her. She crouches on the carpet
stalking with evil emerald eyes
the usurper who has claimed what is hers,
the attention, the affection,
the lap she warms while I work,
her side of the sofa

Perhaps this is why they never last.
Who could feel at ease
with that furry wrath
bearing down upon them, the sculpted brow
and sanded tongue, watching, marshaling
her eldritch incantations
to wrest the interloping gluts from
her side of the sofa.

One never hears of Casanova's cat.
Romeo brought no feline fury to that fateful balcony.

Perhaps it's not the cat.
Could be the charred chicken piccata I cook
determined that this time I will get it right
or the gold-plated Scrabble set,
the giant portrait of the kids on the hearth,
the Judy Garland records—
or something else entirely.
I prefer to think it's the cat.

And late at night
when the children are tucked in and sleeping safely
and the house is lonesome with silence
and I have barricaded myself with
a hot cup of green tea, a puzzle,
a book on the bedside,
and the long tendrils of the sycamore tree
scratch at my window pane
I am grateful for the rumbling goddess
keeping watch on my shoulder.

Shakespeare's Daughter

No one remembers Shakespeare's daughter
the dutiful Susanna who pumped the bellows
and poured the mead. No one recalls
the tireless lass who tended the larkspur
and baked the black bread and wrote long letters
to her absent father. No one knew of the weeks
of preparation for his infrequent visits
only to find him late, or unappreciative, or drunk.
No one helped as she dragged him
to the second-best bed and sang him to sleep
after a long night at Ye Olde Publick House.

Who else knew the scorn of the language arts teacher
at Stratford Grammar, plainly wondering
how this tongue-tied girl could be related
to the immortal bard? Who else bore the shame of
perpetual gossip about dark ladies and swishy earls?
Who else read every word her father wrote
and wondered if she might have inspired
the sharp-tongued Beatrice,
the fair-minded Portia,
the strong-willed Katherine,
or the desperate Ophelia.

One day she would marry a doctor—
I forget his name—
and have children of her own.
How it must have pained her to learn
that not all children are like her
and no one sings for the nightingale

and no one tends the shepherd
and no one remembers Shakespeare's daughter.

Wraiths

On winter nights on the tallgrass prairie
whenever a new child is born
the wind blows cold
the moon holds water
and the dead rise
shimmering, insubstantial
made of memory and smoke
they hover above the yellow plain
waiting

You can ask them questions.
What of my beloved?
When will my time come?
and if you are unfortunate
they will answer

In time they will leave the prairie
in search of the newborn soul
they drift to fields, farms, towns
and where you live
perhaps they are with you now
but whether they are there this moment
or the next
what is important is that you understand

Quailing

"Would you like to fire the rifle?"
"No."

The Sugar Daddy flew through the trees
the secret antidepressant
incongruent yellow on matted forest leaves.
Minnie and Ouchie pointed
the guns fired, birds scattered, birds fell.
Sometimes, if they were not quite gone
my father would bash their heads against a rock
until they were.
I could see how he envied his friend because
his son always tried to please, even when
it was beyond his reach.

"Would you like to fire the rifle?"
"No."

My father whirled and fired and brought down
the idling bobcat with a single shot.
"Did you see that?" he asked, no doubt
hoping for the appreciation
his willful son would never provide.

The other boy was impressed.
The taxidermist mounted it with
its teeth bared and claws unfurled as if
it were about to attack.

III.

"Would you like to fire the rifle?"
"No."

But he pressed it against my shoulder
anyway, showed me how to hold it and
when I would not, forced me to pull the trigger.
The recoil knocked me on my butt
and my father laughed like I had never
heard him laugh before as did
his friends and, of course, the other kid.
I have not fired a gun since.

My mother did her best
but the meat was thin and stringy
and I could swallow a bite.
I would rather have the Sugar Daddy
but it was far away and forever lost
like everything else that day.

Percy

He shivered in my arms as he died
just as he shivered when I found him
abandoned in a field, his whiskers and body
seared by cigarettes, infested with fleas.
I took him home and held him all night long
eventually he told me his name was Percival
but I could call him Percy.

Many people passed through that house
but he said he would always be my cat
and I did not doubt him.
Long hours I spent typing, his body
spread across my wrists, his head bobbing
with each keystroke.
It didn't look comfortable
but he didn't seem to mind.

The shivering ceased as he did and
I whispered that he had been a very good cat
and I would not forget him and I
am embarrassed to say that I was slow
getting him to the vet because I could not see to drive.

For My Rutabaga Baby

I love you as a mailman loves a rutabaga
that will bloom in the tuning fork he once
purchased while rushing out in a hailstorm
to collect the morning tennis racket. I love you
as a spelunker loves a doughnut, casting
candy canes into the surf of Taipei.
When I see you I am crazier than a doorknob,
shinier than a show store, sillier than a soda.
To be near you, I would juggle across
a coffee cup, braving the seeds of
intercontinental pomegranates. Our hearts are
like two cows in a cumulus cloud, managing
their portfolios with an eye to the leafy exterior
of Italian shoes. I believe in you, your tender
street crossings, your loving papier-mâché peanuts,
your ionized and crepuscular pleasures.
None of which makes sense, but what do you
expect when the world has so clearly shifted
on its axis and thrown me into a parallel world
where I can have dinner with you without
drooling on myself (much) and
what about love ever made sense anyway?

My Holland

Windmills are everywhere
twirling ceaselessly in their centrifugal ballet
pumping water out of the canal
providing energy efficiently and inexpensively
as might be expected from the people who gave us the phrase
"Dutch treat."

Farmers pass by
their wooden shoes clitter-clattering on the cobblestones
wearing hats like boiling pans turned upside-down.
They wave and smile.
The natives are friendly.

Although the weather is perfectly clement,
Hans and Fritz sail by on silver skates
and the little boy takes his finger out of the dike
long enough to give me two thumbs up.

Van Gogh makes an appearance.
He is with Rembrandt and his women
drinking pots of coffee and laughing.
They offer me a stroopwafel, but I decline
concerned about my sugar intake.

This is a good place; it embraces me
and distracts me
from the black horizon.

The Historian

So many books
and so many years
searching through glens and hollows
for the last bootlegger
the unadulterated eyewitness
new meat
ingress to an old subject
wading through dusty archives
allergies rebelling
praying for the undiscovered item
a lost detail, a striking graphic
suitable for the dust jacket
yarns not yet yarned
so people can see
what they have not yet seen.

How long before it happens?
The breakout, the turning
point, the defining moment
when I am no longer haunted
by phrases like "nominated
for a Pulitzer Prize" and "It's
just a book, kiddo," the
gravel in my voice grows
with the grit in my eye
I care about people, not
just my subjects, and before I
reach retirement age
I would like to see more
than the eighteen good-hearted souls

who have come today
to Barnes & Noble.

Found Poetry From Leicester Square

I'd be mad if my boyfriend said I smelled.

My dad won't get me sunglasses but he'll get me sunblock.

I told you I didn't want meat pizza. I hate meat pizza.

HE'S OVERFED, OVERWEIGHT, AND OVER HERE!

Can you not move any faster? I'll die of old age before we get out.

When you told me what you told me, I thought you meant it.

Sir Webber isn't fit to paint Stephen Sondheim's toenails.

I can see two different Pizza Huts without turning my head.

THEATRE TOKENS—THE IDEAL GIFT—SOLD HERE

I've never liked meat pizza. Not since the day I was born.

I think the pigeon's name is Benjamin. (It is possible that I misunderstood this one because the woman spoke in German.)

No one really likes cilantro.

Just pull the meat off and pretend it's cheese pizza.

OPENED BY HER MAJESTY THE QUEEN 22 DEC 1992.

There never was a Moses. I heard it on the telly.

I can't tell if I'm still alive.

Would you please just eat the bloody pizza!

Is he writing down what you said?

Deck Party

The woman in the billowy black dress loudly
says she will sit by herself so
as not to bother anyone.

It is her way of asking to be invited to join
their little conversation group.
She will not be invited.
She is too broad, too other
and she is not married so
she will sit alone, occasionally
exchanging words with the handful of other women
who have lost their husbands
or never had them.

The youngest woman has been accepted.
The other wives were reluctant, and
remain guarded, but the husbands
have warmly embraced her, as does her spouse
who is at least thirty-five years her senior.
They are more forgiving, or perhaps
she represents something to them
a spark they do not want to relinquish
or fear has been extinguished.

"Ford is up two-and-a-half points," remarks Fred of Chicago
obviously uncomfortable with so much free time.
"I never gamble," replies Linda, who is celebrating a birthday
at least fifteen years earlier that her actual one.
"Who will get sick next?" frets Pamela.
"The weak ones," Fred answers, adding

"Bank of America is down a half
and the Cubs lost."

The conversation inevitably drifts to better days
the Golden Age
which always seems to be when they were in their teens
or perhaps twenties.
The good war.
Proper rules of courtship.
Hard work, lower taxes.
Wives at home, vacuuming in pearls.

"I think women are better off now than they ever have been."

She is met with silence.
Her husband stirs, shifting his weight, and she realizes
she has endangered her tenuously extended membership.

"I might vacuum more," she adds, quietly, "if I had a better string of
pearls, Fred."

She laughs, and the men laugh with her
because they want to believe that in truth,
that is what all this hugger-mugger comes down to.
She has saved herself
by becoming what she hates most.

The English Countryside

seen through a rectangular train window
becomes an irresistible three-dimensional painting
a traveling Constable that cannot displease
because it never remains the same.

Tempest

The biergarten is empty.
Only last night there was
a relaxed revelry
muted, yet distinctly happy and
filled with the tranquility brought by a cloudy, cool evening
and large quantities of beer.

Now it is morning.
Only a few passing joggers are present
and they do not look as if they are enjoying themselves.

I left the card you gave me on the blue deck chair
because you did not mean it
and I did not want it
and the revels now are ended.

It rained
and the red bled the blue.

After Meeting J.M. Coetzee

In my dream
I am the Nobel Prize winner
and he is the quiet admirer at the foot of the stairs.

He is decidedly modest about the popularity of his work
just as I say nothing about my recent raves in the Utne Reader
and Granta.

I am with a woman named Genevieve
(pronounced the French way).
She is tall and slender and wears a black dress
slit between the legs
pearls and a diamond pendant
and her eyes tell everyone in the room that she adores me
while he is with some bimbo from the hood named Darla
wearing open-toed sandals and capris.

My books are displayed in hermetically sealed library cases
along with literary memorabilia
and a few choice photographs from my distinguished past.

Some of the guests attending the reception
tell him that they bought his latest book
for a hospitalized aunt
or a black sheep brother who didn't go to college.

I am generous when I meet him
and say how much I admire his work
though I don't.

Our lady friends size each other up
and he and I exchange a long transporting look.

He realizes that although our paths had much in common
I am envious of his popularity
just as he resents my astounding success
in the faculty lounge.

"What Happened While I Was Away?"

No matter how long I've been gone
or what occurred in the interim
the answer is always the same:
"Nothing much."

Just once I would like to hear:

"It was a good time for us, Father.
We missed you, but the absence
of a paternal influence forced us to dig
deeper within ourselves and to attain a
level of self-realization I would not
have thought possible during my previous
five years of life."

or

"The babysitter went mad and
attacked Harry with a butcher knife.
He tackled her like a linebacker and
knocked her to the floor, while Alice
used shambitzu--the deadliest of the martial arts--
to subdue her. Ralph called 911."

or perhaps

"All day I felt a certain electricity in the
air, a portent that something of great
moment soon would occur. Then all at once
there was a crackling of thunder, the sky

was riven, and a radiant column of light
descended from the heavens. A voice
speaking in all languages announced that
the End of Days was upon us, divine wisdom
would be granted to all mankind, and the secret
of eternal peace would be revealed.
It involves ice cream."

But instead, their attention
wandering, they say:
"Nothing much."

Though if I seem especially needy,
Alice will add, "How was your trip?"

And I will answer: "Fine."

Valentine's Day

The human heart is nothing like a valentine
symmetrical undulating curves
culminating in a razor-sharp point.
Is love in the undulation
or is love the razor?

Aristotle believed the heart was the locus
of our emotions. He was wrong. Again.
Just as he was about spontaneous generation
and the Sun orbiting the Earth.
The brain leads us astray
releasing those lovely endorphins
that cause us to believe
we have something called a soul
that exists apart from our bodies
that there is life after death
that we don't feel pain
even when we are in love.

The Grinch became a hero
when his heart grew 3x larger
something that would probably not be
a welcome event outside of a cartoon.
Did this make him stronger
or more vulnerable?
More heart to love or
more heart to break
after the Whos have stopped singing
that dreadful song and the Grinch must return
to his lonely cave on that windswept crag?

I didn't want to get together tonight anyway
got it?

This is the trouble with love and valentines.

Paulette

We hover throughout dinner
a witty bon mot, a quotation
from the sonnets, a well-told
anecdote
pelicans skimming the surface
of the water
but never touching it.

William Harrison

I am nothing like you!
reminding me of the many times I thought
exactly the same about my own father.

Don't use that voice!
I hate that voice!
reminding me of all the nights I cradled him
whispering "Annabel Lee" and Hamlet's soliloquy
until he fell asleep.

You're ruining my life!
reminding me of our countless hikes
through that undeveloped lot
he wearing a safari hat, and me pretending
my nose was a compass.

I'm feel like I'm going to explode!
and I recall how he would jump on my back
unexpectedly
and hug tight till he was practically a part of me
and I a part of him.

I must go to the mall!
and as we prepare to cross the street
I reach for his hand
and have to stop myself.

Bug

You learned me
with your tentative touch
and cautious kiss.
I didn't think it was possible
to be more anxious than me
go figure
When we're together
the whole is less than the sum
of its parts
There is more outside than in
we mask the windows
seal the doors
Stuff newspapers in the cracks
but no one can block it all
and so we only dance
when it is dark

My Greatest Poem

I thought of a poem so fine it would short-circuit the Apocalypse
bring terrorists to their knees, weeping
stop war, famine, pestilence
cause the drunk to put down his bottle
and the anorexic to eat
serve as a GPS for the lost and alienated
clear the bag lady's brain
start everyone reading poetry again
and end rap music for all time.

Never again would anyone torture animals
or cheat on their wives
or make children cry
and we would finally see an end
to the greatest of our troubles
which is not war, or famine, or pestilence
but loneliness.

For lo! I have brought glad tidings of great joy.

But I can't remember how the poem was supposed to go.
I touch my Pilot G-2 liquid gel cap to the page
but it only smears.
The roar of the fluttering wings returns
and I can't get it back.

All I can remember is that it ended, thus:
The heart has room enough for everyone.

Visions

I would like to see P.G. Wodehouse
win the Nobel Prize, posthumously.

I would like to see Las Vegas
freed from investment bankers
and returned to the mob.

I would like to see more ice cream,
worldwide.

Parental Conduct Orders should be enforced,
thus: In the event that one parent
bad-mouths the other in the presence
of the children
her tongue will fall out
her face will be covered with pustulous sores
and her forehead will be branded
with a tongue-wagging emoticon.

I would like to see CGI technology lost,
forever.

I think everyone should live in Maui,
taking turns, in an orderly fashion.

I would like to see Jessica—
the Friday night waitress at the hotel diner—
slip into my room
and whisper breathlessly that she is overcome with passion
aroused by my Scrabble skills

and challenge me to an all-night session.

I would like everyone in the world to stop fighting
and I think this could be accomplished
with more ice cream.

I want the thumping in my chest that is not my heart
to stop.

I wish that somewhere in the bowels of the British Library
they would discover a lost Dickens novel
then you and I could dine at Rules
Chateaubriand for two
while discussing the implications of this manuscript
on Chuck's larger body of work
and the various themes presented:
man vs. nature
man vs. society, and of course
man vs. British cooking.

I would like to revisit the summer of '81
when I saw everything for the first time
hadn't spoiled it yet
Ellen liked me
and the Pieta was so stunning
I could not tear my eyes away.

While time-traveling, I should also enjoy
a look at that sixth-grade baseball game
when I hit a triple
and driving home, his eyes fixed on the windshield
my father said
"Well, that wasn't so sorry."

And just for one night
I would like us all to be together
gathered around the game table
children laughing, pizza flying
everything exactly as it should be.

Alexithymia

It isn't really a party when you're
the only one there. I heard someone
snoring—turned out it was me, and where
did all the people go? Don't ask me how I feel
I don't think in those terms it never
leads to anything good where did that
bruise come from and what happened
to my shorts? The television anchorman
is babbling incoherently why
can't he speak proper English? I can't
understand a word he's saying this
would be a good time to finish that
biography of Elizabeth I except it's
hard to focus this early in the morning but
why do the clocks say it's four in the
afternoon? Am I the only one who
knows what's going on? And
stop asking me how I feel I stopped
that a long time ago get in touch with
my feelings who the hell wants
to the only ones that bubble up are
unpleasant and buried for the
same reason you would bury
a corpse. If this were a scene in a
movie the camera would be going
Wah-Wah! in and out of focus to create
shared disorientation. Coppola would groove on
this story it's dark with lots of room for
showy camera bits Gary Oldham smashes
a mirror—how many times have we seen that?—

a bit dramatic and the symbolism is
obvious and cliché where's Juliette
Binoche? Surely we're more than ten
minutes into my movie the love interest
should've been introduced I'm not going
to drink at all today well maybe one
who's going to play me in the movie?
Curly, Larry, or Moe? I vote for
Shemp he's the sensitive one and I
wish you would stop asking me that
stop spinning the room around and
scowling I feel fine!

The White Bird

I open my eyes
and the white bird wakes with me.

He spreads his wide wings
and my heart flutters.

I rise and run
thinking that if I move fast enough

I can escape his fearsome talons.
Children, work, the dreams of others

distractions

always the bird is perched just behind
watching me

beating its wings with rage
when I least expect it.

Nectar

I haven't heard your voice in twenty years.
Was a time I heard it daily
the soft sibilance, the near-lisp
the charming mispronunciations
dispatches from the Zeta house
chipmunk cheeks and impudence and
a surprising capacity for the naughty.
Irresistible smile.
My parents loved you
so did I.

You were determined to make a difference
leave your imprint on the world
far better than any silly storyteller
could hope to do.
Your journey took you to far-off lands
far-flung folk
funky relationships.
I lost you, we all did
and I worried, as the years passed
and the echo of your voice grew faint
that you had lost yourself.

We were so unbelievably young
I had you when everything was
possible, when we had
all the time in the world, and
nothing seemed certain.
How different might it have been
or not

if we had met after, later, now
when our brows are creased with certainty
instead of only tasting your nectar
the heady Icarus rush
in a matrix of flux
before we flew.

No Horizon

The sky and sea merge so perfectly
one flowing into the other
no line of demarcation
it is beautiful and confusing
like a sprinkler in the rain
a world without borders
a dangerous place to live.

Lori

My crimes were the lead story again.
She gave it two minutes
    with bullet points.
The second story was a homicide
    some guy who immolated his brother.
He got twenty seconds.

We're both crazy, dangerous, bereaved
when she called, she said, "I don't want
    to add to your pain..."
and then she did, for three days running.
They told me recovery would be the hardest thing
    I've ever done
but no one warned me about news readers
    on a mission from God.

I have swum too far from the shallow end
    carrying too much
my legs are lead, my hands
    cold and raw and
the current is pulling me away from the shore.
My life and I have broken up.
We're seeing other people and

the fridge is full of food that is not food
    the television with news that is not news
politically correct is neither
    like military intelligence
    and porn actress.

We cannot escape the laws of physics:
  everything decays.

Malibu

From the in-patient balcony
on this fog-shrouded November morning
mist rises from the hills
scorched black by fire.
Barbie lived here?
I hope she escaped safely
collected Scooter, reconciled with Ken
and never had to confront the demons
that must torment
a perfectly sculpted image.

The crows cackle
the fog thickens
I hear the ocean I cannot see.

Birdsong

in the depth of the fog
in the midst of the mist
the piercing creature call
the lost flightless flutter
the one left behind

why it calls, chirrup breaking
where and who but the cry
never reaches the shore
the hummingbird no longer
happy to hover

sometimes it's easy to forget
that even the flightless bird
is carried to shore
by the proper storm

The Oklahoma Kid Rides Again

Deep in the tallgrass prairie
somewhere off the Chisholm Trail
a lone cowboy—
a rustler, really—
herds his cattle, fires
his six-guns, concocts
tall tales for fun and profit
and casts his eye toward the sage.

Come nightfall
he burns his last pot of coffee
cleans his spurs, smokes a cheroot
skims that Ned Buntline he
has read so many times
then lays his head against his saddle
to rest.

The quiet never comes.
He sees a thousand colors in the stars
he sees faces, wraiths
whispering
watching
wondering why.

Moments before sleep, he
closes his eyes tightly and addressing
he's not sure who

or what
prays: I don't need much.
The cattle are dozing.
There's water in the canteen.
A fire crackling.
Just see me through another day.

II.

Something is wrong this morning.
The Kid falls off his faithful stallion
again and again and again and
realizes he is utterly
trampled, destroyed, lost
and it is his own fault.

In a wild delirium
he recalls another life
there's a woman, young'uns
and a mangy mutt who follows him
everywhere he goes.
For a moment he is unsure which life is real
if either
or which he would prefer.

He is there a long time.
The sun beats down on him.
The skin peels away from his face.
He seems to melt into the sand.
There is not much left.

III.

The trail is long and
he's broken and
not sure he can finish
before the weather turns cold
and stays that way.
His coffeepot is dented
his saddle torn, his stallion lame
he has his yarns and himself
Is that enough?

The vultures have picked his bones clean
he hurts and bleeds, covered
with sores and welts and blisters
and he dies, many times, but

. . .

the scratches
whisper to him
the voices
of the children
the white bird
flailing its wings
they cry out
the power of love is greater
than spite and hunger and
long after the sun has set
he puts his foot back into the stirrup.

Baden-Baden

As it turns out, the Black Forest
looks nothing like Black Forest cake.
And the gambling resort town of Baden-Baden
looks nothing like Las Vegas, thank God.
Men do not wear shorts in the casino,
hairy legs shouting, "Show me the eight!"
The only sex shop—Erotik World—is discretely tucked away on a
    side street,
not advertised on a video monitor larger than the state of Rhode
    Island.
And there is not a Starbucks on every corner.
Yet.

The others in my group say this is just like an American resort town,
a tourist trap, which snares the unsuspecting
with offers of soft ice cream and bottled water
that will restore your youth.
But they are wrong.
Where is the venture capitalist
as proud of his swelling belly
as he is of his adolescent wife
with her high-pitched giggle, blonde ringlets, and denim short-
    shorts?
Where are the other captains of industry,
the ladies of the evening?
Where is the young father with the baby carrier on his back?
or the mother herding her enormous go-forth-and-multiply brood
the sullen teenager clutching a skateboard
the elderly couple holding hands as they return to the KOA
Kampground

the high roller who is secretly
a middle-management operations officer at a cardboard box factory
the alcoholic artist
the Elvis impersonator?

It feels good to get away from what is familiar
to force yourself into a new environment
to think new thoughts in new places,
I muse, as I sit at a table in the ice cream café
recalling the life I have left behind
and the faces
and wondering if there is really any difference
as I wait for the rest of the group to arrive
at the Baden-Baden McDonald's.

The Problem with Poetry

In the mountainous Annapurna region of Nepal
a small nine-year old boy goes to work at the rock quarry.
He will earn the equivalent of one American dollar per week.
He will work fourteen hours a day, every day.
His knees will bleed from the toil.
He will not complain.
He knows his dollar will bring a smile to the face
of his beloved mother, who works harder and longer,
and that is enough to carry him through the day.

In the mist-shrouded Argentine rain forest
a young man fights to save a tree.
He knows the tree is special although he cannot explain why.
Perhaps its leaves contain the cure for cancer
or at least a facial cream that will take years off.
So he chains himself to the tree, making it impossible
for them to cut down his friend
without cutting down him as well
and hopes the man operating the bulldozer will care.
Life chained to a tree is slow
and there is never enough to eat
but he has a cause
and that is enough to carry him through the day.

On the frozen moon of Jupiter called Titan
spindle creatures made of glass skitter across the ice.
These ethereal beings communicate telepathically
except for one, who insists on the
freedom to express himself creatively
by moving that tiny aperture between his marble nose

and porcelain chin.
He is an artist, of course.
He has been banished for his heretical vulgarity,
condemned to wander for all eternity
(for the people of Titan never die)
through the barren Ice Forest.
The days are long and lonely
but he has his art, his voice,
and that is enough to carry him through the day.

On a luxury cruise boat in the south of Germany
I sit, pen in hand, confronting the challenge of the blank page,
thinking of my pain, my struggle.
I am hungry
And the deckhand brings me tarte flambeau.
I am cold
and the steward brings me a blanket
and a cup of hot chocolate
with two marshmallow dollops dancing on top.
I am bored
and the program director brings me an accordion player,
and that is enough to carry me through the day.

The Moment She Said "Yes"

my shirt is hideously wrinkled
and half-untucked
but I resist the urge to fix it
noticing that my forest green polo shorts
with double pleats
and a button fly
held up by a braided burgundy belt
do not remotely match
the bright white sneakers
I kicked off ten minutes ago
furthermore

the air conditioning has ramped up
making goose pimples appear
on my hairy legs
and trembling arms
solidifying my belief
that I am experiencing coronary thrombosis
at this most inopportune moment
and then

she takes my hand
and all my fears
and my wrinkled clothes
dissolve
and I am glad to be rid of them

DNA

"Watch me kill the zombies."
"Say these lines, I'm making a movie."
"I made you a hobo on Wiki."
"I changed your profile pic to look satanic."

I am completely lost.

He is everywhere at once
and nowhere to be found
cuddling the cat, catching the frog,
climbing the tree, so infused with energy
living life completely on his own terms
that my sleepy eyes recall a shade...

(dancing to that Winnie-the-Pooh record
performing comic strips on the diving board
posing for pics with a powderpuff
reciting Night Before Christmas on the hearth
singing so loud the rafters rattled)

...before "There is only one correct choice" and
"You're acting like a girl" and
"Do you want to suck hind-tit all your life?"

DNA is a starting block, not a finish line
and you are a kid, not a clone
when I see the electricity in your eyes
I know you will save trees
and grow tomatoes, scuba-dive,
sail around the world, help

those in need, compose masterpieces
or not
as you choose
from infinite possibilities.

The only life you need lead is yours.

Fair to Poor

"How can a guy who is so good at
being friends with women be so bad
at dating them?" Barry asked, after
I described my last failed first date.
"In front of an audience of five hundred
      you're fantastic.
At a dinner table for two...
      fair to poor."

It happens thus:
The date goes well until the first time
      I am required to speak
      and downhill from there.
"You look lovely this evening"
and immediately I can see from her expression
that I have said something wrong.
Is it too soon to comment on physical appearance?
Does it sound like a come-on?
Did it imply that she didn't look lovely
      on some previous evening?
I try to correct my gaffe, only making it worse.
"Of course, you always look lovely"
which sounds like a line, even to me.
From that point, I evaluate every word
before speaking it, at least twice.
This conversation does not go well.
There is no second date.

"You should only be allowed to date
women you don't like," Barry declares.
"If you like her, you get
nervous and screw it up. Lower the stakes."
He suggests the services of a hypnotist
to make me believe I don't like her
before the date begins. Then I might
be able to get to the appetizer
        without stuttering.

The post-hypnotic suggestion could be rigged
to disappear when I hear the words:
"I had a good time. Let's do it again sometime."
And the chances of a second date
would improve slightly...
        from fair to poor.

Tons of Time

You have tons of time, my father said.
No rush. Europe is expensive, especially
now. You're too young. You won't
appreciate it. You won't remember it.
Stonehenge isn't going anywhere. Casting
rune stones only creates fear. And I seriously
doubt it was an ancient UFO landing strip.
Tons of time.

I did get there but these days
you are only allowed to see Stonehenge
from a distance.

I have tons of time, I explained,
to develop a personality. For now,
I must focus on my work. I'm an artist.
Not a performer. Not a damned
trained seal. I write for eternity.
After-dinner amusements are rubbish.
I can be charming later. An artist has priorities.
I have tons of time.

But now I have crossed the middle marker
and it turns out that easy only seems so
from a distance.

We have tons of time, you tell me.
Only fools rush. There are so many
questions. Things you don't know.
It takes time to build a relationship.

We must be patient. It's not my nature
to rush. I've been burned before.
True love doesn't happen overnight.
We have tons of time.

I wish that time were endless, when I'm with you
but when I cast the rune stones I can only see you like Stonehenge
from a distance.

Idylls of Baast

He used to lie across my typing wrists
as if it were the most comfortable place imaginable.
I was his Disneyland
the happiest place on earth;
he was my orange and white comforter
and I did not mind the extra weight
it did not slow me down.
I created new worlds with six fingers
buffeting his furry head in the process.
He seemed content. He would close his eyes
and rumble with soft engine sounds

and dream of the place from whence he came
the place where he belongs
the place where he and his people reign supreme.
He is good to his subjects
occasionally giving them his enigmatic glance,
the cushion of his paw,
and they give him the tribute he commands.
He is a benevolent ruler
concerned, proactive
but at night he flies
high above his kingdom and into the midnight blue sky
soaring across the vast ocean
dotted with islands ruled by his feline brethren
freed from the duties of administration
or the strictures of the cage, however
pillowy and indulgent
no longer dependent, no longer
tied to the trivial expectations of humanity.

He is there now.
I can see him, his silhouette in the starlight.
He is more than content
and I am comforted
by the knowledge that he has found his tribe
and is free at last.

Parallax

In high school science we
learned that you can identify any
point in space if you have three coordinates.
Triangulation fixes location
in the time-space continuum, somehow providing
an informing perspective. Could it
permit other insight
I wonder.

Many years ago I was in
Montana which they call Big Sky
Country for damn good reason.
One night I watched the Pleiades meteor shower.
Ursa Major was on the left and Polaris
was on the right and at the highest point I saw
a thousand shooting stars
and I knew what I wanted to do
and I was filled
with wonder.

Last night we floated through
dinner and you looked more radiant
than Polaris on its best day.
A couple desperately in love
got married to our right and another
became engaged on our left
there was something new in their eyes
and the Statue
of Liberty was just ahead

and I couldn't help
but wonder.

AIB, 13

I was prepared for the Awkward Age
the physical changes, personality,
frustration, exasperation, even rage—
but not for this.

I was prepared to smile knowingly, thinking
This too shall pass.
And we will always love each other, I tell myself
as much as it is possible to love anyone
right?

You are in your room, alone, with a book.
Who showed you how to read?
Seemed like a good idea at the time.
My questions are greeted with
monosyllabic replies, grunts,
eye rolls, withering glares, sarcasm—
the lowest form of human discourse—
and finally the screaming:
Why can't you just leave me alone?

Here's why:
I still remember reading you Charlotte's Web
taking you for long walks in the rain
through the San Juan Mountains
hand-in-hand
watching you sneak downstairs after bedtime
so we could watch Buffy the Vampire Slayer
coming to the choir loft
midway through the service

so you could sit on my lap.

The Awkward Age is supposed to be
awkward for you, not me. I should
be the parent
but instead I'm a marionette
with tangled strings, a poor sap trapped
in Shelob's web
and you are the elusive hummingbird
who hovers in midair for a short time
and then skitters away
faster than my eye can follow.

Abecedarian

V is for Vacant
W is for Wanting
X is for Extraneous
but not really.
Y is for "Why not?"
Z is for Zacharias
or Zedekiah.
We learn letters
to give shape to the intangible void
and to distract ourselves.
A is for Aching
B is for Blunder
C for Catastrophe,
D for Delirium.
There's an abecedary of danger out there
We must armor ourselves
from the calamitous capitals
and the insidious smalls
We must convince ourselves
with the random array of Fs
also Rs and Ts and Os and especially Js
that we are filled with
possibilities and not simply
V is for Vacant.

Gratitude

The falcon never thanks the falconer
who gets too much credit anyway
and never even leaves the ground.
The piano never thanks the pianist
but still enjoys being played.
And I don't need to thank you
even though you made this time work
made it bearable
made it unique.
The blue light isn't something conjured
it's you.

The ocean never thanks the shore
especially when the ocean
stretches forever, and the shore
is full of footprints.

I miss your smile most of all,
then your enthusiasm, then your voice,
especially reading your poetry
but I don't need to thank you
because I was just the piano
and you are the pianist
and you always will be.

These Days

When I see a tree these days
I see it for you
as if should I look hard enough
you might see it too.

When I hear a joke these days
I laugh at it for you
as if I might transmit some joy
to help you muddle through.

When I sniff a rose these days
I savor it for you
so we might share the ecstasy
of passionate perfume.

When I take a meal these days
I eat like I'm in famine
because I want you fed and well
and know you love your salmon.

When I think of you these days
I see you ringed in silver.
I wish you were another shade
for nothing rhymes with silver.

When I check the time these days
I do it with some tears.
This time apart is much too hard
and measured in dog years.

Physics Lesson

When the sun grows cold
and the fire of the heavens is quenched
and the comets end their travels
The moons quit orbiting
and the planets form no more
No more revolving, no more rotating
no more primordial soup
And the expanding universe ceases its journey
When the sky is black
and the nebulae dark
and not a twinkle is left to recall
what came before
When there is no light, no life, and no time
and nothing to be seen as far as the eye could see
(if there were an eye to see)
You will still be loved
and I will still be true
because even though the world is finite
and time is fixed
and the universe itself must end
love is eternal.

Morning Poem

You fell asleep in my arms last night
I know
I heard the sweet susurrus of your breath
so light at first, then deeper
as you fell further into your well-earned release
who knows what movie Morpheus played
the flutter of your eyelids might signal surprise
and the tiny shudder a plot twist
you radiate heat
your sweet osmotic warmth
reminds me that each day is dear
and life is good
because you fell asleep in my arms.

Inventory

On the last day of the decade
    it seems appropriate to make a list
    of that for which I am grateful
Such as the woman
    who first heard rhythm in language
    and marked it down in ink
And also the child
    who first tried to capture clouds
    in oil infused with color
I honor the first troubadour
    who found structure in air blown through hollow reeds
He who first found a marble slab
    and imagined Venus
Or saw a sparkling stone
    and used it to bring a loved one delight.

I revere the visionary who took desire
    and jealousy and need
    and transformed them into love
That was our greatest invention
    the one that gave meaning to all that had come before:
    the musician's song, the painter's scape
    and the wondrous stirrings
    the desire and want and poetry.

Pupukea

Forty-foot waves crashing against volcanic rock
    with foam so white it becomes milk
    Poseidon's bubble bath
    the snow of the tropics

Infinite valley, trees touching the stratus
    reluctant weeds that shrink from your approach
    purple flowers, all the more exotic because
I do not know their name.

This is the jungle of a thousand secrets
    I can hear it whispering

The parliament of trees is one of those trying cliques
    that tell you they heard some gossip about someone you know--
    but it would be wrong to tell you what it is.

The horses and the wild pig on the boy's back
    a luau in the making
    the rainbow rarely touches down on the other side
    and the pot of gold is not tenure, hairdos
or a perfect credit rating.

Pupukea stills the soul
    quiets the bird
    the niggling questions about purpose

And the effervescent wish that the endgame
    be about something more than winning.

Sonnet 1

"I love you" are the words he says but still
A questing mind may wonder what it means.
So this is what's conveyed when spoke by will;
To vanquish doubt I thus spell love's machines:
It means that even when the worst winds blow
You know there's one who's always on your side.
There's one who'll take your hand should sickness show;
When you need someone most he will abide.
This puts on you *en plateau* with those most dear:
The generation last and that to come.
Through tempests fierce or falseness, failure, fear,
You know you never need face life alone.
This is as true as if were sworn in court,
So now you know these rare words' true import.

Sonnet 2

Absence makes the plaintive heart love best.
That's the Sunday sage's word and wish.
The inverse of clichés about houseguests
Familiarity and rotting fish.
But my love swells regardless of locale
Intensity is heaven's burning beast
Unyielding passion is its rationale
It smolders when there can be no release.
There'll come a time you'll find my feelings changed.
Perhaps you feared the love might stultify?
As time makes seasons spin and life deranged--
Each day you'll find my feelings multiply.
This is my pledge; and not just poet schmaltz
No time will come when you will find me false.

Sonnet 6

This pit, this hole, this hell is not so great
As all the black that now surrounds my soul.
Its gravity permits me no escape;
My gaoler is myself, my fiercest foe.
The greatest gift I ever got was you
This treasure I should horde instead I hurt
With madness and all reasoning askew
My finest jewel is ground into the dirt.
I've always said what now self-serving seems:
That partnerships are love's hard-etched endeavor.
It's tempests' trick to test the lovers' dreams
So weathering this, we reach into forever.
Whatever secrets Time may hold in store,
My love and life are yours, eternal, yours.

Sonnet 7

We cannot waste a single second's sum.
I've waited so long just to see you near,
Felt panic from the call that didn't come
And diagnostic countdowns too severe.
Time expands in your vicinity
And shrivels when you whisper each goodbye;
Each day we're one provides serenity
I choose to take them always by your side.
Let each day start with seeing your sweet smile
And end there too, and let me be succinct:
Together we will blaze across the sky
The meteor that made alone extinct.
I ask you now to always warm my side
Bid love return each morning in your eyes.

Love's Labour Regained

Sunday before the holiday
you and I were at the garden
with the patron and the man in charge.
We'd left the giant shuttlecocks
behind for cattails and
lambs' ears and
the flowering plants of the season.

Any fool could see we were in love
transparent as a bedroom window
naked in our blues.
Peer deeply into my eyes and
see us dozing, waking, dozing
your hand touching mine
as if by instinct.

We posed for pictures by the Japanese maple
stroked the sleeping pussy
admired the heliotrope and hydrangea.
We held an orchid in our hands
and our hearts.
The garden was all in bloom.
It had not seen the first winter.

Fiction Writing

If we were a novel
would it be a coming-of-age story,
a redemption saga, or
a testing plot?
I think the male protagonist needs
    some character development.
Forget about the three-act structure
    we need many acts, endless acts
    so we never reach the denouement
    but follow one climax with another
    and another
    and another.
The premise is unique
    the antagonists readily apparent
The dialogue fresh and witty
    and the descriptions of the love interest
    crackle and pop like peanuts
    on a marketing director's desk.

The term "love story" is passé
    there's no audience for that
    in these enlightened times
Except
I wonder what some readers would give
    for the tiniest taste
    of the plot we're unraveling.

How to Get Published

The focus should be on the garret
every writer needs a garret
messy, yes, but not too.
This is a workspace, after all.
A few piles of wadded paper
    that's enough
perhaps an empty pizza box
and a very stale cup of coffee.

Ritual is everything
You will need your special writer pens
an appropriate reclining chair
so you can prop your feet up
    as you gaze out the window
your special writer blanket across your feet
your special writer kitty in your lap.

Watch for those characters who come to life
    and take control of the story
Less work for you.
Make the most of unpaid laborers.

Be sure the laundry is washed
    otherwise, this is hopeless.

And perhaps when everything is just so
and your inner eyelid is open
take just a moment to figure out
    what you want to say.

Rapture

The anticipation of you
is the rapture of the intangible
the brass ring almost within reach
the fine wine ordered but not yet tasted.

The nearness of you is the breath of possibility
the musky trace of exotica
the hint of nirvana
the white bird at rest.

Hope is not the thing with feathers
eternally poised to escape
but instead the thing with Velcro
that merges with your soul
filling the sweet lacunae
between what you want and what you wish.

All I want now is the slow approach of the Nissan
the straightened hair
your arms spread wide
the rapture of the tangible.

23

the shriek from the roller coaster
the gasp of recognition
the touch of an unseen feather
the anticipation of your name being called
the knife darting from off-screen
the first step into a darkened home
the forest of fairy tales
every time I see you

Drift

Deep in the dark all the dead and the dying
rise from their beds both above and below
walk if they can, drift if they cannot
hearing the strain of the song from the rock
zeroing in upon it.

They come from all over, from every which way
their faces well-worn but the light not yet lost
the light merely dimmed, and then as they gather
the collective shine can be seen from afar
and also from within.

They cannot know what has brought them together
they cannot know what they're hoping to find
they're seeking the cure; they are not optimistic
but it's there all around and always has been
if only we could see.

My Finest Hour

They have come from everywhere.
John and Yoko are in the front row
       (Harry brought them in a taxi)
Everyone I have ever known arrives
       and thousands who only know me
The critic sits discreetly in the center
       scribbling into a notepad
       "One doesn't like to attract attention."
My parents retreat to the wings
       Uncertain

The mayor has given me the key to the city
       he remarks upon my phoenix act
       throws rose petals at my feet
The president sends his regards.
A UN resolution declares a day of rest
       so that all may observe
CNN provides live coverage
       the signal is broadcast worldwide
       translated into all languages
Martin Scorsese plans a concert film.

Nothing like this has ever happened before
       least of all to me
The mood is anticipatory and electric, filled
       with whispers, heavy breathing, darted eyes

The curtain rises.
The stage dark, the world silent.
Then the klieg lights blaze.

I sit at the Steinway and smile
     wearing my best Armani tux
        with the red Converse sneakers
The stage is bedecked with Stratocasters
        amps, speakers, ProTune
        and this capo I really like
A mike squeals. Commentators are puzzled
        they have no advance script.

And then at last
        I close the lid over the keys
        step atop the concert grand
        spread my arms wide
And sing the song you taught me.

Acknowledgements

Some of the poems included in this collection have previously appeared, in some instances in altered form, in the following publications:

"My Finest Hour," and "#23" — *Pegasus*, Vol. XXXIII, Spring 2013.

"After Meeting J. M Coetzee," and "AIB 13," — *New Mirage Journal*, Winter 2012.

"Shakespeare's Daughter," "Alexithymia," "The Historian," "The Professor" -- *Conclave: A Journal of Character*, Autumn 2012.

"Wraiths" – *Rose Red Review*, Summer 2012

"Scratches" – *Weinberg Memorial Library Newsletter* – Fall 2010

"What Happened While I Was Away?" – *Caveat Lector* – Winter 2008

"My Holland" – *Language and Culture* – Winter 2008

"Deck Party" – *Caveat Lector* – Winter/Spring 2008

Author's Note

I want to express my gratitude to Balkan Press and particularly my editor Savannah Thorne, who waded through a messy file of poetry and unearthed the ones she thought might make a good book. She has a keen eye for language, and a strong red pencil for the unnecessary. I made so few changes to her selections and arrangement that they are not even worth mentioning.

I also want to thank my family, particularly my mother, who assiduously saved the poems I wrote when I was seven, all of them bad enough to end a career before it began, my best friend and sister Karis, the subject of many of those poems, and my children, who have mentioned that it is bad enough that they're in my novels without being dragged into my poetry.

About the Author

William Bernhardt published his first two novels in 1991, a crime novel called *Primary Justice* and a literary novel called *The Code of Buddyhood*. He has since published thirty-two more books, including the popular Ben Kincaid novels. Bernhardt is also one of the most sought-after writing instructors in the nation. His small-group seminars have educated many authors now published by major publishing houses.

Bernhardt holds a Master's Degree in English Literature from the University of Tulsa and is a two-time winner of the Oklahoma Book Award. He is the only writer to have received the Southern Writers Guild's Gold Medal Award, the Royden B. Davis Distinguished Author Award (University of Pennsylvania) and the H. Louise Cobb Distinguished Author Award (Oklahoma State), which is given "in recognition of an outstanding body of work that has profoundly influenced the way in which we understand ourselves and American society at large." In addition, he has written plays, including a musical (book and music), humor, nonfiction, children's and young adult books, biography, and crossword puzzles. He is a member of the Author's Guild, PEN International and the American Academy of Poets. This is his first book of poetry.